Date Due

OCT 22 MAY 16 1987		
OCT 10 NOV 10		
NOV 24		
DEC 8		
MAY 8 SEP 26		
Oct		
MAY 20		
SEP 18		
OCT 8		
NOV 18		
DEC 20 1974		
SEP 20		
SEP 29		
JAN 22		
FEB 20 1992		
NOV 03 1994		

1918: GAMBLE
FOR VICTORY

THE MACMILLAN BATTLE BOOKS
are prepared under the general editorship
of Edward R. Sammis

Special maps drawn by Harry Rosenbaum

1918: GAMBLE FOR VICTORY

The Greatest Attack of World War I

By ROBERT COWLEY

THE MACMILLAN COMPANY, NEW YORK
COLLIER-MACMILLAN LIMITED, LONDON

© The Macmillan Company 1964

All Rights Reserved

First Printing

The Macmillan Company, New York
Collier-Macmillan Canada, Ltd., Toronto, Ontario

Library of Congress catalog card number: 63–16753

Photo Credits: Brown Brothers, pages 9, 14–15, 78; The Bettmann Archive, pages 3, 16, 26–27, 34–35, 38, 46, 86; Hearst Photo Library, pages 25, 81; National Archives, title page; Radio Times Hulton Picture Library, pages 4, 11 (left and right), 13 (left and right), 18–19, 23, 37, 49, 53, 56, 58, 60, 65, 76; United Press International Photos, pages vi, 30, 44; Wide World Photos, pages 41, 72, end papers.

Designed by Hilda Scott

Printed in the United States of America

Contents

British tank rolling through a devastated village in France

First Days of the War

For the common soldier, subject to the horror and sacrifice of prolonged mass warfare, no struggle in history can compare to the First World War.

It lasted four and a half years—August, 1914, to November, 1918—and cost almost ten million lives. During that time, the imagination of man, capable of so much good in normal times, became obsessed with one monstrous end: to reduce killing to an exact science. Some of his inventions of war had been used before, but never with such deadly effect. Others were new and more fiendish than anything yet conceived.

There were machine guns (developed in our own Civil War) that cut men down by the hundreds, like scythed wheat. Massed artillery fire from the most powerful cannon yet devised sought them out in their pitiful hiding places and tore their bodies apart with methodical precision. There were airplanes that bombed and strafed them from the sky, and submarine torpedoes that struck at them from under the sea. Tanks ground them into the shell-torn earth. There were poison gas, too, that ate away their lungs, and liquid fire from flamethrowers that charred their bodies into cinders of unrecognizable flesh. That man could perpetrate such horrors is to his lasting discredit. And yet, that he could endure them for so long is an awesome testimony to his courage, and to his will to survive.

Today, nearly fifty years after the last gun was fired on November 11, 1918, World War I seems remote and unreal. Yet it altered our lives as few events in modern times. Old nations ceased to exist. New ones were founded. Empires that once ruled the earth fell into permanent decline. Out of the ruin of war, tyranny was bred: Fascism in Mussolini's Italy, Nazism in Hitler's Germany, Communism in Stalin's Russia. There could have been no World War II without World War I, nor, for that matter, a Cold War.

Unlike the Second World War, and more recently the Korean War, the war itself was not a clear-cut clash of differing political systems. It was not a matter of Democracy against Fascism, or the Free World against Communism. Nations went to war essentially for reasons of national pride. They fought to determine what territory rightfully belonged to which country, and who had the biggest army or the strongest navy, and who would be the industrial leader of Europe and the world. As each of the great powers tried rigorously to outstrip the others, an armed showdown became inevitable.

When the war came, it came so suddenly that men did not have a chance to think or reflect. They were simply swept along by circumstances over which they had no control. On June 28, 1914, an assassin from the tiny (and now extinct) nation of Serbia murdered the heir to the Austrian throne. Austria-Hungary retaliated by invading Serbia. But Russia stood behind the Serbs; feeling her interests threatened, she declared war on the Austrians. This, in turn, brought in

Austria-Hungary's ally Germany, and Russia's ally France. It remained only for Germany to invade France through neutral Belgium, a country that England was pledged to defend, and all of the major European powers were involved.

On their side the Central Powers were led by the aggressive young German Empire and her shaky partner, Austria-Hungary. Among the Allies, France and the tottering giant that was czarist Russia were the first to fight. Britain had the support of what was then her Empire, including Canada, Australia, New Zealand, India, and South Africa. Later, Italy and the United States joined the Allies.

In those first days, everything was sweep and movement, and men were enthralled by what they fancied to be the grandeur of war. Russian armies dashed across Germany's eastern boundary, and were promptly and disastrously ejected. German forces swung in a great wheel through Belgium and France, and reached the suburbs of Paris before they were thrown back to the river Marne. Then trenches were dug, shallow affairs meant to be used only for the shortest time. In that fall of 1914, it still seemed that the war would soon be over. But winter followed, and as one year of stalemate and slaughter succeeded another, men despaired of winning. They merely burrowed deeper into the earth that was their only protection.

*Dugouts in a
French hillside*

CHAPTER ONE

The Western Front

The Gathering Storm

March, 1918: the Western Front . . .

The fourth winter of the war was over; another spring had come. In the trenches that scarred the earth of Belgium and France from the dunes of the North Sea to the mountainous Swiss frontier, millions of war-weary men faced each other along 445 miles of battle line.

To the men in those trenches, this was a struggle that would never end. But at least the winter—one of the worst in memory—with its snow and sleet and freezing mud, was over. Sunny days and milder temperatures lay ahead. Shoots of new green appeared in the wastes of no-man's-land that separated the two lines. Birds sang from the branches of blasted trees that stood like skeletons on the landscape. As the days grew warmer, the only reminders of winter were the ominous mists that blanketed the ground each morning, sometimes so thick it was impossible to see more than a few feet in any direction.

On the Allied side of the line that month, men were uneasy. Rumors flew: a great German offensive was coming; no one knew just where, no one knew when, but some time very soon. Later, survivors would remember feeling a vague dread that made them restless, a numbness at the pit of their stomachs that they could not shake.

Day after day, Allied intelligence reported vast movements of enemy troops and supplies, the building of new railroads, hospitals, airfields, and gun emplacements. The Germans were planning an attack on such a scale that they could hardly hide their preparations. In one spot British observers noted mounds that looked at first glance like large haystacks extending for several miles at one-hundred-yard intervals. These were forward ammunition dumps. Although the Germans made a show of intense activity against the

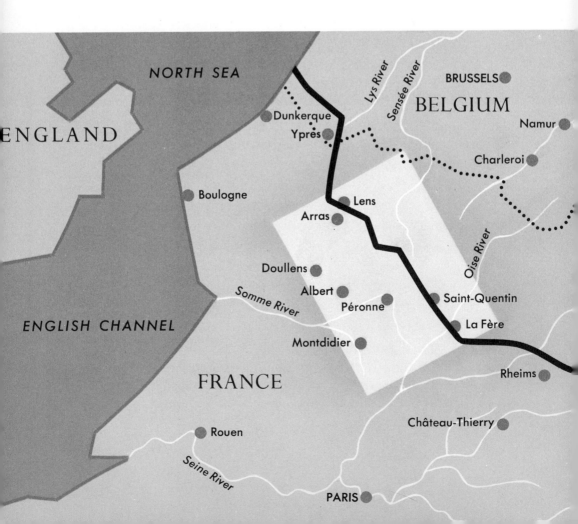

French in some sectors, evidence pointed more and more to an attack along the British front, which at the time ran for 126 miles, almost from the North Sea, through the small wedge of Belgium still held by the Allies, and down through the northwestern corner of France to the Oise River.

During the day, everything seemed quiet. Beyond range of enemy rifle fire, an occasional rugby game, tug-of-war, or a boxing match was enjoyed. Artillerymen lolled by their guns in the sunshine.

With the coming of night, the mounting pressure became evident. The air was filled with thunder and the earth shook, as big guns dueled with high-explosive shells. Men worked

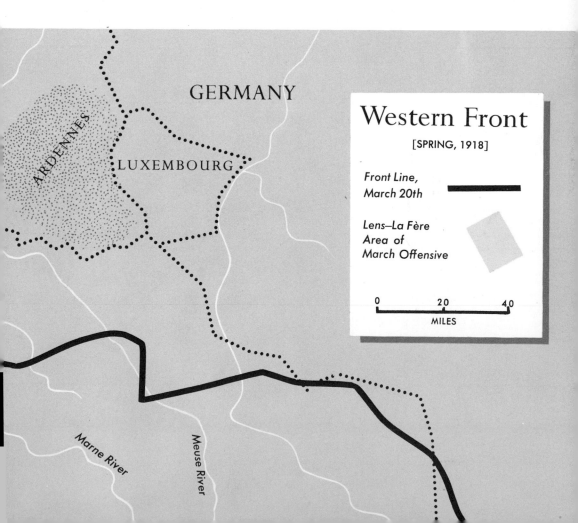

GERMANY

ARDENNES

LUXEMBOURG

Western Front
[SPRING, 1918]

Front Line,
March 20th

Lens–La Fère
Area of
March Offensive

0   20   40

MILES

Marne River

Meuse River

furiously, laying barbed wire and telephone lines, digging trenches and shoring up the small circular strongpoints, called redoubts. Under cover of darkness, ammunition was brought forward, and heavy cannon were manhandled into position and camouflaged under heavy burlap screens or netting covered with leaves and branches. Every evening, from one end of the front to the other, patrols crawled out into the moonlike craters of no-man's-land to watch and listen for signs of suspicious enemy movements. As white star shells or the flares called Very lights burst like Roman candles above their heads, machine guns raked the earth in set patterns, searching for these patrols and sometimes catching them, helplessly exposed.

There were also trench raids. In these brutal, close-quarter encounters in the dark, men fought blindly with a variety of weapons. They clubbed wildly with spades and rifle butts. They fired pistols, machine guns, rifles, and occasionally a sawed-off shotgun. They stabbed with bayonets, squirted liquid fire from flamethrowers, pummeled each other with their fists, and hurled grenades. When nothing better was at hand, they used rocks.

The Trenches

By 1918 the continuous front lines of earlier days, with their main strength concentrated in the forward positions, had mostly disappeared. They were replaced more and more by what was known as "defense in depth."

In this new system, developed by the Germans and copied by the British and French, contact with the enemy was maintained only by a scattered fringe of lightly held outposts. The principal function of these outposts was to give alarm in

German soldiers in Belgium during the first months of the war

the event of attack and to harass the initial enemy advance as much as possible. They were to hold out to the last.

Behind this "Forward Zone," at a distance of half a mile to three miles, was the "Battle Zone." Here the real resistance began. The Battle Zone was studded with machine-gun nests and redoubts, each placed in such a way as to support its immediate neighbors. Barbed-wire networks, instead of being drawn straight across the front in a continuous belt, lay at angles, with gaps carefully spaced to lure the attacker into avenues swept by machine-gun fire. Other openings would be raked by the field batteries that lay even farther back—along with more strongpoints, saw-toothed lines of support trenches, and deep camouflaged dugouts hiding large numbers of men waiting to be called into action.

Finally, there was supposed to be a "Rear Zone," referred to as the "Green Line," also heavily fortified. In most cases, however, this Rear Zone, if it existed at all, was little more than a thin scratching of trenches.

This, then, was the tactical situation as the Germans planned their spring offensive in 1918.

The "Robot Napoleon"

Though the Allied generals displayed an outward calm and professed not to be worried about the German threat, they were only too aware that their position was desperate.

The year just ended—1917—had been a disaster. Repeated offensives had failed with heavy losses.

Germany's military leaders were perfectly content to let Britain and France batter away at the Western Wall. The more the Allies attacked, the more they weakened themselves, which was all to Germany's benefit.

The Germans enjoyed a temporary advantage and they planned to make the most of it with a great spring offensive.

The strategy for the attack was conceived in the mind of General Erich von Ludendorff, working in close cooperation with the German General Staff, one of the most efficient military organizations in all history.

Ludendorff was the man for the job. Although he bore the uninspiring title of Quartermaster General—a title conferred on his deputy chiefs of staff by Field Marshal Paul von Hindenburg—he was, for all practical purposes, top man in the German Army, more powerful than the aging Hindenburg himself. Cold, calculating, and wasteful with human life, Ludendorff was a brilliant strategist with a long string of victories behind him. He knew superbly how to manage

GENERAL
FERDINAND FOCH

FIELD MARSHAL
SIR DOUGLAS HAIG

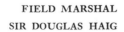

the great conscript armies at his command. Sometimes it seemed that he was not a man at all, but a smooth-running and ruthlessly efficient machine. One historian has characterized him as the "robot Napoleon." He despised the rule book and established a reputation as a nerveless gambler who made the surprise move his trademark.

He faced his biggest gamble now.

Meeting with a small group of high-ranking German officers on November 11, 1917, at the Belgian town of Mons, Ludendorff worked out with the officers the general plan for the offensive. Neither Kaiser Wilhelm II, ruler of the German Empire, nor Field Marshal von Hindenburg was in attendance.

Events in the weeks that followed seemed to confirm the wisdom of his decision. The Russians on the Eastern Front were completely broken both by a succession of German victories, achieved for the most part by Ludendorff himself, and by revolutionary upheavals culminating in a Communist take-over. For all practical purposes, they were out of the war. This defeat was made official by the treaty of peace with the Central Powers, signed at Brest-Litovsk on March 3, 1918. Thus, hundreds of thousands of fresh troops were made available to Ludendorff for his offensive against the Western Front.

Ludendorff, however, must have seen that time was running out. The period of his advantage was short-lived. The gamble had to be taken soon.

While the armies on the Western Front were locked in a stalemate, Germany itself was on the verge of collapse. Slowly, surely, the four-year naval blockade was strangling her to death. Food and fuel were almost impossible to obtain. Long lines of weary, half-starved women and children stood

FIELD MARSHAL
PAUL VON HINDENBURG

GENERAL
ERICH VON LUDENDORFF

shivering in the mud and snow of city streets as they waited for meager rations of flour or sugar, or a few bones for soup. Some sort of explosion seemed inevitable. In January, 1918, disorders broke out. They were quelled only by the intervention of the army.

More and more people at home were demanding a peace settlement. They asked: "Why not quit while we are ahead?" But the generals were in control, and nothing less than total victory would satisfy them. The enemy must be so completely crushed that Germany's dominance in the

world would be assured for many generations to come.
There was not much time.

The United States had entered the war in April, 1917.
While it had taken time to raise, train, and equip an army,
the first troops of the American Expeditionary Force were
already landing on French soil. They would continue to
come, in ever-swelling numbers, to man the trenches along
the Western Front. The British and French armies had to
be beaten decisively before fresh American troops reached
the Allied lines in force—or the chance would be lost forever.

*Aftermath of a food riot
in a Berlin street*

CHAPTER TWO

Preparations for a Spring Offensive

The Target

Ludendorff decided that the attack would be made against the British. He reasoned that since they had assumed leadership of the Allied cause, they must be destroyed first. It seemed likely, in that event, that France would give up without waiting for the Americans.

Geography also entered into his decision. The French had an almost unlimited amount of space behind them in which to withdraw, while the British had almost none. The sea was always at their back.

But which sector of the British front would he strike? At first Ludendorff favored an attack along the northernmost fifty miles, roughly from the border of France and Belgium to the North Sea. Here British forces were most heavily concentrated, and here they were dangerously close to the coast.

There was one serious drawback—the Flanders mud. Any drive on those soggy flatlands would have to wait for the earth to dry. And he could not afford to wait. So Ludendorff shifted his plans for the attack to another part of the British line, the region between Arras and Saint-Quentin. Here higher ground and harder earth did away with the problem of mud, making possible large-scale troop movements in the early spring.

Moreover, with its open plains rolling away monotonously in every direction, the countryside offered few natural obstacles. There was little to relieve the eye. One might see an isolated cluster of ruins marking the spot where a village had once stood, or a row of poplars, stiff as bayonets, lining a lonely road. Several rivers, including the Somme and the Oise, meandered through shallow, marshy valleys, but they were neither very wide nor very difficult to cross.

However, there was one major obstacle. Ahead of the advance lay a vast wasteland, forty miles wide and seven miles deep. In the spring of 1917, retiring after the Battle of the Somme, Ludendorff had ordered a systematic destruction of everything in the area that the enemy might find useful. Roads had been torn up, forests chopped down, drinking wells poisoned, and entire villages dynamited. If the German offensive centered on the Somme area, Ludendorff would now have to pass over the same ground.

All this Ludendorff took into account. And yet, one particular consideration made an attack here too tempting to resist. It was in this sector that the British and French linked

*German column
advancing across
Somme battlefield*

up—a loose connection at best. The two allies wrangled constantly, and cooperation between them was almost unheard of. Sometimes one would carry out an attack without even bothering to consult with the other. Ludendorff suspected (and with good reason) that the French might be less than eager to come to the aid of the British if they felt their own interests endangered.

Then, in the middle of January, an unusually valuable piece of information reached the German commander. The French, it seemed, had badgered the already shorthanded British into relieving them along an additional twenty-five miles of trench line. The French and British argued fiercely, and the French premier, Clemenceau, threatened to resign. In the end the British consented, and reluctantly extended their line southward from Saint-Quentin to La Fère, on the Oise River. It was a decision they would come to regret bitterly.

The extension of the British line, moreover, would be occupied by an army with a reputation for bad luck—the Fifth, commanded by General Sir Hubert Gough. Its losses had been the heaviest of the four British armies on the Western Front. This unfortunate army took over from the French a line that was in a sorry state of disrepair.

Paris in April?

Ludendorff's plan was as grandly conceived as it was bold. Three German armies, numbering almost 800,000 men, would smash forward along the forty-three-mile front, from Arras to Saint-Quentin to La Fère. This would be as large a force as had ever been assembled for a single battle. Once having broken through, the two armies on the German right flank would wheel *to the northwest,* and push the British back to the sea. The connection between the French and the British would be broken. Meanwhile, the army on the German left flank was to move forward *only as far as the Somme River.* This attack would be mainly a holding action, to repel any counterattacks that might menace the northern advance from the rear.

The offensive was to begin at dawn on the 21st of March. Ludendorff's staff gave it the code name "Michael."

Three other attacks would follow shortly afterward, but only if "Michael" bogged down. Ludendorff confidently expected that it would not. Still, he was taking no chances. The second, called "Mars," would hit the fortified city of Arras, pinning down the British in the area while "Michael" battered at them from the flank and the rear. Two further attacks on the front in Belgium would fall on either side of the exposed Ypres salient, squeezing it out in a pincers movement. The British line would be torn away from its anchorage on the sea, and rolled up remorselessly.

"It will be an immense struggle," Ludendorff predicted in a letter to the Kaiser, "that will begin at one point, continue at another, and take a long time; it will be difficult, but it will be successful." He was, he said elsewhere, prepared to lose a million men in the effort. But—whatever the cost—he expected to be in Paris by April.

Battle Tactics and Weapons

One great problem remained to be resolved. Ludendorff counted on immediate advances of twenty-five miles or more. But if the Allies had never yet been able to forge such a breakthrough, how could he?

To begin with, he proposed to use artillery in an entirely new way. Instead of a methodical preparation lasting for days, the attack would be preceded by a sudden, short, and utterly devastating bombardment that would throw the enemy off balance. Every foot of the British front line would be scoured by shellfire.

Great reliance would be placed on that most fiendish of World War I weapons, poison gas. It could contaminate vast areas without cluttering them with impassable crater fields, and existed in many varieties: tear gas that blinded; mustard gas that not only blinded, but painfully blistered the skin; phosgene gas, which, with its fatal delayed effect, weakened the heart and often felled men two days after they had breathed it. Most dreaded of all was chlorine gas, which ate away the tissue of the lungs, so that men died, suffocating, as they tore at their burning throats with their fingers and gasped for air.

The brief but intensive artillery preparation was to be followed by a novel form of infantry attack known as "infiltration." No longer would there be the long, closely packed lines of attackers moving shoulder to shoulder in one wave after another, to be mown down by a few resolute machine gunners. Now, small picked units called "storm troops" were to lead the advance. Armed with light machine guns, trench mortars, and flamethrowers, they were to penetrate—or "infiltrate"—the enemy defenses as rapidly as possible. When they found the weak points, the storm troops would flood through them.

Contrary to past practices, reserves would be thrown into battle, not where the attack was held up, but where it was moving forward. They were to widen the gaps the storm troops had opened, mopping up in their wake, and leapfrogging them if fatigue and losses brought them to a halt. Whatever happened, the fastest, not the slowest, must always set the pace.

With great speed and secrecy, his mighty offensive took shape. All movements of troops and artillery were carried out at night. In many cases, assault divisions were held back until the very last moment, to give them needed rest and to hide their presence from the British. "Safety officers" supervised all lines of communication, censoring letters and monitoring telephone conversations.

If Ludendorff could not hope to conceal the time and place of his attack, he could at least hide the size and extent of it.

Pillbox on a ridge south of Lens

On the Line

The 20th of March came. Tension mounted. The Kaiser had arrived at Ludendorff's headquarters at Avesnes-lès-Aubert. In the forward trenches men moved into position, overflowing the dugouts and crouching close-packed behind the protecting earthworks.

Ludendorff's troops were filled with optimism. One young officer recalled: "All the roads were crowded with columns on the march, eagerly pressing forward, with countless guns and endless transport. Woe to any unit whose movements were not up to the scheduled time! They were ruthlessly relegated to the ditch and had to wait hours before they found a gap into which they could squeeze."

Now it remained only for Ludendorff to give the final order to begin. For a moment he hesitated. The weather had turned wet, and a continued downpour might spoil everything. Rain and a wind blowing in the wrong direction could prevent the use of poison gas. But there was no stopping the operation at this late date. As he wrote of that last frantic day: "Every delay must have increased the difficulties of troops crowded together close up to the enemy. Already the tension was very hard to bear. . . . Everything must run its course. General Headquarters, senior commanders, and troops had all done their duty. The rest was in the hands of Fate. . . ."

In the early hours of the morning of March 21st, a dense fog crept up, enveloping the entire front. Men found themselves shivering as much from cold as from fear of sudden death. Waiting impatiently for the bombardment to start, Ludendorff took the fog as a bad omen. Would it hold up his attack and give the outnumbered British a chance to beat

off the German onslaught? Perhaps. But it was useless to
worry now. . . .

And what of the British in those tense last hours before
the storm broke?

It was, on the whole, a quiet evening. Along most of the
front a thick mist began to rise just before dark; a chill rain
fell. Because of the bad weather and the limited visibility,
only a few raiding parties went out that night, but what they
found was cause for alarm. Everywhere the Germans had
cut gaps in their own wire, presumably to let their attacking
infantry through. The scattering of prisoners taken by the
British talked openly about the great offensive about to begin

British trench covered with barbed wire on the Western Front

in a few hours. All of them were anxious to be sent to the rear: they did not want to be caught in the British front line where they might come under bombardment of their own big guns.

Some British divisions manned their battle stations immediately. Men in forward positions drew lots or volunteered to crawl forward to the isolated observation posts beyond the front lines, each carrying with him a Very pistol. When they saw the enemy coming, they would fire the green flares that would warn the troops dug in behind them that the attack had begun.

So the night wore on. The rain stopped. For one moment, the skies cleared and stars could be seen. Then the fog swept in again. Four o'clock came and went. Men glanced at the luminous dials of their wristwatches. Four-thirty. Along the trenches ran a clicking sound as men cocked their rifles.

British troops in a forward position in the Battle Zone, armed and waiting to meet the great "Michael" offensive on March 21st

LUDENDORFF'S GAMBLE FOR VICTORY

SPRING, 1918.   Europe's future is to be decided in this small part of northern France. General Erich von Ludendorff has massed the strength of the German Army along a forty-mile sector running from Arras to La Fère. He plans to break through the heavily fortified British-French line in one spine-crushing blow, separating the British from the French. He will then roll up the British line in a drive to the North Sea. Thus he hopes to annihilate the enemy and march on to Paris.

To accomplish this he has already increased his strength on the Western Front from 146 divisions to 192. Hundreds of thousands of additional officers and men come fresh from the recently collapsed Russian front, and from other battlefields of Europe.

He plans to concentrate his attack at one point. For this largest assault in history, he has 800,000 men to draw on, organized into 62 massive divisions.

CROWN PRINCE RUPPRECHT'S GROUP.   The Seventeenth Army, under Otto von Below, and the second, under Georg von der Marwitz, will exert the main force of the attack. First they will cut off Cambrai. Then the Seventeenth will swing to the northwest to seize the well-defended town of Arras. The Second will continue directly westward, halting its left wing along the banks of the river Somme.

GERMAN CROWN PRINCE'S GROUP.   Oskar von Hutier's Eighteenth Army will strike south of Saint-Quentin. Gayl's four divisions of the Seventh Army will attack at La Fère. The main objective of both armies is to offer cover and support for the striking force north of the Somme.

In a modern war a general does not win simply by outguessing the enemy's plans or by acting boldly. The enemy is too powerful, and too tightly massed. Ludendorff feels that he must concentrate on finding a weak point in the enemy line. If he finds it, he can break through quickly. Before it can be reinforced, he can destroy the enemy's line of communications, and put his artillery out of action. His success depends on the strength of his attack, and his ability to continue the advance.

Ludendorff tours the front in January. He finds the weak spot. On January 21st he decides to strike in the Saint-Quentin area, where the French and the British lines are only loosely joined. He issues the necessary orders to mass for the attack.

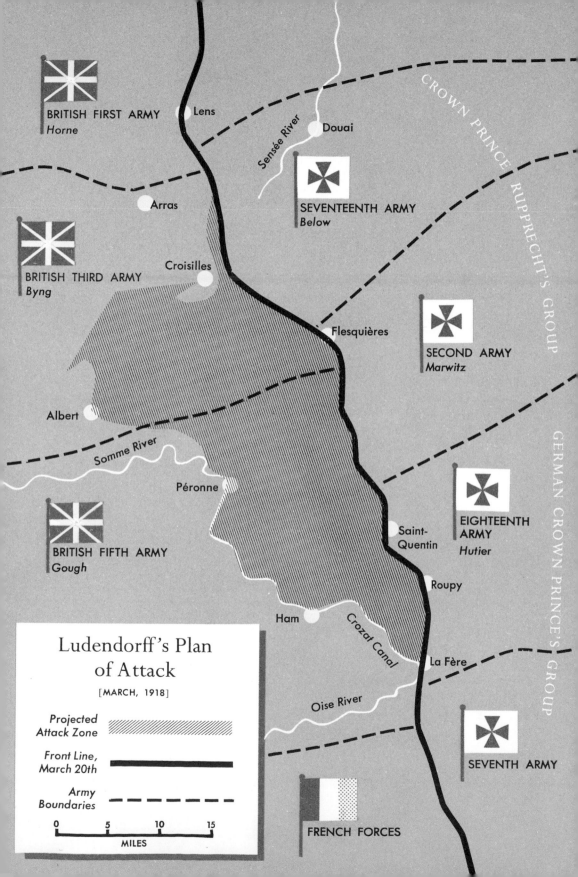

BRITISH FIRST ARMY
Horne

Lens

Sensée River

Douai

SEVENTEENTH ARMY
Below

Arras

BRITISH THIRD ARMY
Byng

Croisilles

Flesquières

SECOND ARMY
Marwitz

Albert

Somme River

Péronne

BRITISH FIFTH ARMY
Gough

EIGHTEENTH
ARMY
Hutier

Saint-
Quentin

Roupy

Ham

Crozat Canal

La Fère

Oise River

CROWN PRINCE RUPPRECHT'S GROUP

GERMAN CROWN PRINCE'S GROUP

SEVENTH ARMY

FRENCH FORCES

Ludendorff's Plan of Attack

[MARCH, 1918]

Projected
Attack Zone

Front Line,
March 20th

Army
Boundaries

0   5   10   15

MILES

CHAPTER THREE

The Great Attack

March 21st

At 4:40 A.M., in the cold darkness of the hours before sunrise, Ludendorff's bombardment descended with a tremendous crash on the British line.

Winston Churchill, as Minister of Munitions, had been visiting the front on a tour of inspection. That night he found himself quartered at a divisional headquarters in a ruined village perhaps five miles behind the lines. Except for the distant rumble of artillery fire and the thudding explosions of occasional airplane raids, an eerie quiet had settled on the darkened landscape. Churchill, who knew the attack was coming, could not sleep.

"I woke up," he remembered, "in a complete silence at a few minutes past four and lay musing. Suddenly, after what seemed about half an hour, the silence was broken by six or seven very loud and heavy explosions several miles away. . . . And then, exactly as a pianist runs his hands across the keyboard from treble to bass, there rose in less than one minute the most tremendous cannonade I shall ever hear. . . . Far away, both to the north and to the south, the intense roar and reverberation rolled upward to us, while through the chinks

in the carefully papered window the flame of the bombardment lit like a flickering firelight my tiny cabin."

Churchill dressed and went outside, where he met the general commanding the division. "This is *it*," he told Churchill.
"I have ordered all my batteries to open. You will hear them
in a minute." But the din was now so great that the firing of
two hundred additional guns seemed hardly to add to it.

From the high ground on which he stood, Churchill could
see the front line for many miles. "It swept around us," he
wrote, "in a wide curve of red leaping flame. . . . There
were still two hours to daylight, and the enormous explosions
of the shells upon our trenches seemed almost to touch each
other, with hardly an interval in space or time."

And so it was everywhere. In those first moments, some
six thousand German guns let go, hurling a storm of steel
along a front of more than forty miles. "We were stunned
by the concussion of literally thousands of bursting shells,"
a British infantry officer, Lieutenant Colonel Deneys Reitz
reported, "and although the light was uncertain, for there
hung a mist, we could see that all our front stood wrapped in
a sea of smoke and flame, and the earth heaved and twisted at
our feet." Telephone lines had been smashed by the bombardment, and communication with command posts in the
rear was all but impossible. "We ordered up three signallers
with an electric flashlamp to communicate with Brigade
Headquarters," Reitz continued, ". . . but they were blown
to pieces within ten minutes, and for the rest of the time we
held the front we were isolated, except for some runners that
got through."

Hour after hour the shells rained down, in a never-ending
torrent of hot metal. Trenches and outposts in the Forward
Zone were completely obliterated, and most of their dazed

occupants as well. In the Battle Zone, the German artillery searched out battery and machine-gun positions with uncanny precision. Crossroads were blocked by a relentless hail of high explosives, and ammunition dumps went up in dense, billowing clouds. Even objectives twenty-five miles in the rear came under fire. "It was evident from the outset that the enemy had marked down his targets with considerable accuracy," the British *Official History of the War* commented later. "Divisional headquarters, telephone exchanges, railway stations and other important centres all received hits . . . so heavy was the fire that the very air seemed to vibrate with shell bursts." Key positions were also deluged with poison gas. It mingled in a nauseating and often lethal mixture with the heavy white mist that covered the ground like a shroud and cut visibility in most places to a matter of yards.

Poised in their trenches, German troops watched the scene with mounting elation. Some ran up and down, shouting and joking. Others, with little thought for their own safety, mounted the earthworks and looked on with mixed horror and wonder at the wall of fire and the blood-red clouds that towered above the British lines. Nine o'clock came, the fifth hour of the bombardment. Officers began to group their men and herd them forward into no-man's-land. They took cover in shell holes just in front of the British Forward Zone. In their gas masks and helmets, the German storm troops looked like thousands of gray-clad insects, gathering in great swarms as far as the eye could see.

At 9:35 the bombardment reached a crescendo, the grand finale of Ludendorff's nightmare symphony. Five minutes later, the barrage lifted from the first line of enemy trenches. As desperate warning flares went up from the defenders—a useless gesture, since they could not be seen in the fog—the

German infantry stood up and charged in a great wave that battered and crashed upon the whole of the stunned British line from La Fère to Arras.

The Charge

For the Germans, that onslaught began exactly as planned. Well-trained storm troops rushed forward through the gray, rolling smoke, the attacking waves of infantry bobbing up and down in ghostly lines over the broken ground. Many carried portable trench mortars, light machine guns, and flamethrowers; most still had their rifles slung, preferring to use in those first moments the stick bombs they carried by

the fistful and had stuck in their belts. "In my right hand I gripped my revolver," one young German lieutenant remembered, "in my left a bamboo riding cane. I was boiling with a fury. . . . The overpowering desire to kill winged my feet. Rage squeezed bitter tears from my eyes."

What happened next has been vividly described by Barrie Pitt in his book, *1918*. "The main assault troops," he writes, "moved fast as they had been trained to do. . . . Aided by the fog, they passed quickly through the forward positions, evading the known isolated posts and redoubts, jumping across the trenches when they came to them, finding their way by compass and memory of well-conned maps or often of the ground itself when they had fought across it before.

Behind them, the second and third attack waves mopped up—sometimes by merely directing dazed and bleeding prisoners of war to the rear, sometimes completing the havoc of the guns with bayonet and rifle butt. Where organized resistance remained, they encircled it, but if its reduction proved too difficult or too lengthy, the task was handed over to the follow-up divisions and the artillery."

Death in the Trenches

The storm troops pressed onward. As they began to probe the Battle Zone, British resistance gradually stiffened. From the maze of zigzagging trenches, dugouts, and redoubts, British rifles and machine guns opened up by the hundreds and thousands. Artillery joined in, pouring shrapnel and explosive upon the attacking hordes. Now it was the Germans' turn to suffer heavy losses, though they hardly seemed to be slowed by them. Their infantry fell upon the British like men possessed. They hurled stick bombs wherever a head presented itself, and squirted streams of liquid fire into dugout entrances and hidden machine-gun emplacements. They ran to and fro among the shell holes in search of one enemy after another.

As adversaries clashed in close combat, strange and dramatic meetings sometimes took place. There was, for one instance, the experience of a German officer named Ernst Junger. Making his way along the shell-pounded hollow of a sunken road, he came suddenly upon a wounded British soldier, crouching in front of him. Junger's first impulse was to kill, and yet he hesitated.

"I saw him start at the sight of me," the German wrote, "and stare at me with wide-open eyes as I walked slowly up to him holding out my revolver in front of me. . . . Grinding my teeth, I pressed the muzzle to the temple of this wretch, whom terror now crippled, and with my other hand gripped hold of his tunic. With a beseeching cry he snatched a photograph from his pocket and held it before my eyes . . . himself, surrounded by an enormous family. . . .

"I forced down my mad rage and walked past."

Moments later, Junger found himself in an enemy trench. Stumbling around a corner, he collided with a British officer. He seized the man by the throat and flung him against the wall of sandbags, where he collapsed. Just then, one of Junger's senior officers appeared behind him on the rim of the trench and shouted above the din, "Shoot the hound dead!"

German cavalry moving through the ruins of Saint-Quentin

But Junger did not. As he commented grimly: "I left this to those behind me. . . ."

Such was the nature of these trench struggles, which were all the more brutal because they were fought in such a confined space. German soldiers remembered firing down that day into trenches that seemed to be seething with Englishmen, and throwing bombs in their midst as they tried to scramble away. Hundreds jumped out and ran for their lives in the open, where they were savagely cut down.

"They stumbled over each other as they fled," Junger related, "and in a few seconds the ground was strewn with dead. Only a few got away." Others did not try to escape, but raised their hands above their heads in a gesture of surrender. Often, in the heat of battle, these men were shot with the rest.

Almost a million men took part in the first day's fighting. Perhaps twice that number became involved before the struggle finally subsided two weeks later. Ludendorff launched 37 divisions in the opening assault. Nearly 30 more, 370,000 men, were held in close support and were soon engaged; by the end the number had swelled to 90. The Germans had almost 800,000 troops at their immediate disposal. On the same front, the British Third and Fifth armies could muster only 17 divisions in the line that first day, and five more in reserve—a total of about 300,000 men.

"Taking its scale and intensity together," Winston Churchill wrote in the late 1920's, " 'Michael' must be regarded without exception as the greatest onslaught in the history of the world." Until the campaigns in Russia of the Second World War, it remained so.

For Ludendorff's armies, March 21st was a day of almost unbelievable success. In the valley of the Oise—the southern flank of the front held by Gough's Fifth Army—German gains were especially spectacular. Here the fog seemed to hang thicker than on any other part of the line. Later in the day it dispersed, making the task of the storm troops that much easier. Between Saint-Quentin and La Fère, they had pierced the Battle Zone, and in at least one place were practically through it. British Fifth Army troops stationed far behind the front line were often startled to see hundreds of gray figures emerging from the mist. They barely had time to defend themselves before they were overwhelmed.

Some escaped. Many more did not. One who escaped was an artillery major named Hamilton Gibbs, who commanded a battery four miles to the rear of the Forward Zone. He was so far back that he did not expect to have his guns in action before evening. But as the morning wore on, Gibbs began to receive frantic phone calls ordering him to lay down a barrage no more than a mile in front of him. He could hardly believe that the enemy could have penetrated so far, and in such a short time. And yet, hardly had he given the order to fire when he saw the shapes of men moving forward through the fog. There could be no doubt about it—they were Germans.

Anxiously Gibbs swept his field glasses around once again. What he saw was even more alarming. Another group of the enemy was creeping along a railway embankment that was actually *behind* his position. He directed his gunners to fire first at the Germans menacing the battery from the front. They ran. He turned his guns on those in the rear, and they, too, were disposed of. So it went all day. More attacks came and were repulsed. But it was clear to Gibbs that he and his men could not hold out much longer where they were.

That evening orders came for him to evacuate. What was

left of the British right flank was forming a new line of defense behind the Crozat Canal, which connected the rivers Somme and Oise.

As Gibbs withdrew, the situation was becoming more and more dangerous. The entire Battle Zone between Saint-Quentin and La Fère could no longer be held. In fact, the German forces had broken through the crumbling lines of Allied resistance.

Resistance

Above Saint-Quentin, however, in the center of the line, the situation looked a good deal better for the British—at least for the time being. In some places their men even

Remains of Saint-Quentin bridge after the German bombardment

stopped the Germans in the Forward Zone, especially where the sun broke through the fog early in the day, giving machine gunners a clear field. But their desperate stand cost the British more men than they would be able to replace for days to come.

Meanwhile, at the salient that bulged around the peasant hamlet of Flesquières, the Germans made still less headway. Preferring not to hit it head on, they tried to pinch out the salient from either side, but with little success. As the hours passed, the hardening resistance of this heavily fortified bulge in the line began to assume an ever-increasing importance. It was as if the Flesquières salient was a pillar of granite holding up a line that by evening resembled a sagging roof. Once it went—once Ludendorff succeeded in toppling that pillar, either by frontal attack or by undermining—the whole British line would collapse in the middle.

That the Flesquières salient did not give way that first day may well have saved the British from a disaster of truly major proportions—as if what had happened already was not bad enough—for just beyond, on the northern flank of the "Michael" attack, the Germans seemed on the verge of a breakthrough. Here, division commanders of the British Third Army had made the fatal mistake of packing too many men in the Forward Zone, and the slaughter during the morning's bombardment had been hideous. The German storm troops easily reached the Battle Zone, where the British held on desperately. At one point, the *Official History* reported, the Germans came to a railroad embankment, lobbed bombs over it, and even snatched hot rifles from the hands of the men firing them and surged ahead. There seemed no stopping Ludendorff's hordes that day.

By evening, only a thin strand of trenches stood between

the attackers and open country. As a last resort, the British pressed every man available into service. One brigade of infantry stationed in reserve several miles behind the front was interrupted in the middle of a rugby match and sent up to fight; within hours the brigade had almost ceased to exist. In several cases, cooks, clerks, and batmen—the so-called headquarters "details"—were also called to serve. That afternoon, when a gap opened in the line, one of these makeshift units actually raced German storm troops to reach a disputed position and beat them to it. British airmen played their part, too. Their squadrons, flying recklessly low, strafed and bombed the close-packed masses of German infantry moving up for the attack, inflicting losses that Ludendorff would feel acutely in the days to come.

But, in places, not British gallantry but the Germans' own miscalculations halted their advance. "We were brought to a stop," Ernst Junger complained, "by our own artillery, which had the stupidity to go on shooting at the same spot until the next day." The reason for this, apparently, was that the German guns had not yet been dragged forward. They were firing away at maximum range, unaware that their distant targets now were often their own comrades. But it could not be helped, because in the confusion of battle messages took so long to filter back. No one knew for certain just how far various units had penetrated.

Still, to know the reason for the blunder was small consolation to the German rank and file who saw easy, and perhaps decisive, gains thus denied them. Unable to move forward through the deadly curtain of steel from their own artillery, they could only wait helplessly for the coming of the night.

With darkness, a measure of quiet settled over the scene.

Some who never saw the second day of the "Michael" offensive

The harried British commanders—who knew only too well that it might be days before help arrived—used this brief respite to regroup their shattered forces and somehow improvise new defenses. While this was going on, the Germans moved up their plentiful reserves, and confidently prepared to resume the attack.

All was confusion. Battle lines had become indefinite, and whole units often found themselves stranded deep in enemy-held territory. "Under cover of night," Barrie Pitt writes, ". . . parties of British infantry crept out from shell-holes, from dug-outs and sections of blown-in trenches, to begin filtering back towards their own lines. Platoons—or their survivors—sections, individual men, all moving secretively and intently across the cratered surface, listening for guttural voices, for the grate of the sentry's rifle on the parapet, for the smooth click of the cocking-handle. Sometimes they were caught or killed, sometimes they had to fight their way through enemy positions—preferably with bayonet or club —more often they avoided them. Sometimes, inevitably, they completed their journeys only to be shot by their own compatriots holding the foremost British positions, and taut with expectancy for the renewal of attack."

Frequently that night, British cannoneers hitched up teams of horses and led them forward to rescue precious guns from under the very eyes of the enemy. Elsewhere, cold and weary men merely looked for shelter or something to eat. German soldiers, who had too long endured scanty food rations and a lack of warm clothing, looted provisions from English dugouts, and collected blankets and overcoats from prisoners and the dead.

At dawn on March 22nd, Ludendorff's armies once again stormed forward.

CHAPTER FOUR

The Great Retreat

Collapse

The second day of the "Michael" offensive was in many ways a repetition of the first. But for the British, the situation changed from bad to worse. The fog had returned, to blind and confuse their gunners, and to hide and protect the enemy infantry.

Under cover of the fog, German forces on the southern flank of the attack moved up to the Crozat Canal, which connected the Somme and Oise rivers and gave the British a natural line of defense to fall back on. From there they hurled a shower of mortar and machine-gun fire at the British dug in on the opposite bank. This new defensive position might have proved a considerable obstacle to the attacking Germans. But in the haste of their retreat, the British had failed to demolish completely the canal bridges. Near La Fère, by noon, storm troops managed to pass over a partly blown-up road crossing. Before long, thousands of Germans were pouring into an ever-widening bridgehead.

Here the British found themselves on the verge of calamity. And just to the north, between the Crozat Canal and the Flesquières salient, the Germans had shattered the line.

General Gough's undermanned Fifth Army divisions simply collapsed. They had reached and passed their limit of bravery and endurance that second day. They could bear the weight of repeated assaults no longer. Suddenly, everything seemed to go wrong at once. "The whole of our army machine," an English journalist wrote, "was upset . . . like a watch with a broken mainspring and loose wheels."

Staff officers dispatched orders that were never received. Troops fought in isolated pockets, out of touch with the units around them. Gun batteries shelled their own infantry by mistake. In the chaos men panicked and gave up positions that might have been held. Others retreated to defensive trench lines in the rear of the Battle Zone where they hoped to make a fresh stand. They found these trenches uncompleted or, worse yet, nonexistent.

A Bloody Tale

In his brief but memorable memoir of the March offensive, an officer named Herbert Read told of an experience that was, for British soldiers that day, all too frequent. Read commanded the remnants of a battalion of infantry holding a redoubt near the village of Roupy. Starting in the early morning, the Germans had attacked his position no less than seven times. By four o'clock in the afternoon, the battalion was cut off on both sides and was in danger of being overrun. Read did not know what to do. The sensible move was to retreat, but the one message he received from headquarters merely exhorted him to hold on to the last man. So he held on. Only when it became obvious that the situation was hopeless did he finally, on his own initiative, order a withdrawal.

Word was passed down the line. But it was already too

late. Lying on his belly in a shallow pit, with machine-gun bullets whining over his head, Read watched the bobbing helmets of German soldiers, as the enemy methodically bombed their way forward with grenades along the zigzagging trenches that led toward the redoubt. His men began to crawl into the open, preparing to make a break for safety.

What happened next was a scene of pure terror. "I saw a piteous band of men rise from the ground, and run rapidly towards me," Read later wrote. "A great shout went up from the Germans: a cry of mingled triumph and horror. 'Halt Englisch!' they cried, and for a moment were too amazed to fire, as though aghast at the folly of men who could plunge into such a storm of death. But the first gasp of horror expended, then broke the crackling storm. I don't remember in the whole war an intenser taste of hell.

German infantry advancing from a forward Battle Zone position

"My men came along," Read continued, "spreading rapidly to a line of some two hundred yards' length, but bunched here and there. On the left, by the main road, the enemy rushed out to cut them off. Bayonets clashed there. Along the line men were falling . . . swiftly as the bullets hit them. Each second they fell, now one crumpling up, now two or three at once. I saw men stop to pick up their wounded mates, and as they carried them along, themselves get hit and fall with their inert burdens."

Now he was up and running with his men, their goal a line of trenches some three hundred yards to the rear where he expected to find both shelter and reinforcements. It seemed to take forever to race the distance. "My heart beat nervously, and I felt infinitely weary. The bullets hissed about me, and I thought: then this is the moment of death. But I had no emotions. I remembered having read how in battle men are hit, and never feel the hurt till later, and I wondered if I had yet been hit."

But when he finally reached the line, he relates, he was in for a shock that was, in its own way, almost as deadly as the impact of a bullet: "*The trench had not been dug, and no reinforcements occupied it.* It was as we had passed it on the morning of the 21st, the sods dug off the surface, leaving an immaculately patterned mock trench."

The British Hold Fast

By the evening of the second day, March 22nd, the situation in the center of the British line had grown so desperate that they fought no longer to hold ground but merely to gain time. Some units of the Fifth Army had even retired behind the Somme River, and now found themselves from ten to fifteen miles behind the original front line. In at least two places, great gaps had opened, one of them four miles wide.

Even the redoubtable Flesquières salient now seemed suddenly threatened with encirclement, as the line on either side of it bent in. But once again the pillar remained firm; its continued presence loomed ever more important to the hard-pressed British. As long as the salient held, Ludendorff could not gain the vast breakthrough along the entire front of the offensive that he counted on. And if that breakthrough was delayed a day or two more, the British might get the reserves they needed to slow and eventually perhaps to stop the German advance.

North of Flesquières, moreover, where Ludendorff's men had done so well the day before, Third Army resistance was fast hardening. Reserves were more plentiful here, and in contrast to the south, the rear defensive positions were well prepared. The morning fog for once came to the aid of the defenders, hindering the accuracy of German artillery, which no longer had the advantage of being able to fire at fixed and carefully spotted front-line fortifications.

All through the day Ludendorff, with mounting concern, followed the slow forward progress of his divisions in the sector between Arras and Flesquières. This, he knew only too well, was the exact place where his grand plan of victory might succeed or fail. If his troops did not break into open country soon, the opportunity to make the great wheel-around to the northwest, with its irresistible rolling up of the British line, might be forever denied him.

And so, late that afternoon, in violation of his own principle that attacks should always be pressed at the weakest and not the strongest point in the enemy line, Ludendorff threw in the full weight of his reserves on the north. With a reckless bravery, his masses pushed onward; the British line wavered and then gave way. A six-mile gap yawned open— but by evening it had closed again. At the village of Vaulx-Vraucourt, the *Official History* reported, "heavy fighting ensued in the streets, as men from the divisional reinforcement camp, who were hurriedly digging a line behind, 'downed tools' and made a fine counterattack by which the Germans were driven out." Twenty-five tanks were also thrown into the breach. As they crunched forward, like steel beetles, the German infantry panicked and fled. Once more a decisive victory had eluded Ludendorff; once more his losses had been staggering. That evening, British prisoners watched the Germans remove great clusters of their dead from the battlefield; the bodies were tied in bundles and stacked in waiting carts like chopped cordwood.

Fighting for Time

Nowhere was the British defense more stubborn than on the far northern hinge of the "Michael" offensive. On a low ridge above the valley of the Sensée River, a pair of battered battalions, probably totaling between them little more than a thousand men, held off forces many times their size, and effectively barred the German advance for two days.

Lieutenant Colonel Deneys Reitz, who commanded one of these units, wrote: "Repeated attacks were made and every one of them broke down. We were drenched with gas for thirty hours on end, and they pounded and battered our trenches until we hardly recognized them, but the men who were left clung doggedly to their shattered ramparts and fought on. With the trench in ruins, it was wonderful that anyone survived at all. . . ."

Finally, on the second day, the Germans managed to drive a wedge between the two battalions. Reitz's men found themselves outflanked on both sides, and cut off in the rear by a barrage. When evening brought a lull in the fighting, he ordered a hasty retreat. Except for shovels needed for digging a new line, all supplies were destroyed. Papers and maps were burned. Grenades they could not carry were buried.

As the men straggled back, shells crashed around them. The moon was shining brightly, and it illumined a scene of devastation that had an almost supernatural horror about it.

British cavalrymen passing the once splendid Albert Cathedral

Every yard of earth, it seemed, was torn up. Even redoubts of concrete had been blown to pieces. All low ground lay under a haze of poison gas. Reitz related how "we made our way past broken guns, wrecked gunpits, and dead gunners, all looking weird and ghostly through the goggles of our [gas] masks."

Farther on, he witnessed a sight that, in its touching way, revealed something of the fierce loyalty of the ordinary British soldier. "As we walked, we passed four men . . . carrying a dead officer on an improvised bier, made from a length of duckboarding. The moon shone on the dead man's face. . . . He looked calm and restful, and he might have been asleep, so little was there of death in his countenance." When Reitz asked them what they were doing with the body, one of them told him that they weren't going to let the Germans bury their "skipper." So they were taking him back to a place behind their lines where they could be sure of doing the job themselves.

The Great Retreat

Saturday morning, March 23rd, began as usual with a mist, enabling the Germans to get across the Crozat Canal in several more places. Before many hours had passed, the British southern flank had melted away. In the dense fog, units not only lost connection with one another but all sense of direction. Some became so confused that they blundered into the midst of the enemy. When the haze finally lifted, retreating men often turned to see thousands of antlike figures advancing against the skyline.

They were Germans, of course. . . .

Meanwhile, in the center, Gough had ordered a general

withdrawal behind the Somme River. Perhaps this was unavoidable, perhaps not. At any event, in the hurry and confusion of the evacuation, large numbers of wounded were abandoned, and vast stores of food, clothing, and other vital supplies were lost. The Somme line, too, was doomed. Unfortunately, no one thought to destroy the bridges that crossed the river. This oversight may not have mattered in the end, for a long drought had left the stream so low that it could be easily forded at too many points. For this reason alone it was not much of a barrier to the determined German forces.

Worse yet, the Flesquières salient was giving way at last. Threatened from both sides and almost pinched out, it managed to survive all through that third day and into the night; but at seven o'clock on the morning of March 24th, the decision to retire was made.

So the granite pillar was toppled, and once it had gone, nothing in the world could hold up the rest of the line. The roof had indeed caved in on the British. Thus, along the entire front of the "Michael" offensive, a great retreat (in British history, *the* Great Retreat) began. Where it would end, nobody knew.

Pursuit

Back the British went, back through the wasteland of ruined villages, poisoned wells, and chopped-down orchards that the Germans had left in 1917. Back they went, through the barren, moonlike landscape of the old Somme battlefields. For the hundreds of thousands of men who were swept up in it, the retreat was a nightmare that seemed to have no end. The days were cold, and the nights colder.

British troops on the road to Péronne during the great retreat

Food was almost unobtainable, and anything more than a moment's rest out of the question. Men staggered like drunkards along endless roads. When they lay down to sleep, they collapsed in motionless heaps like the dead. But always they had to get moving again, for the enemy was never far behind. From high ground, British soldiers could see the sausage-shaped observation balloons that marked the German line of advance, bobbing forward in an irregular line from one end of the horizon to the other.

Sometimes the Germans were closer than anyone thought possible. Early in the retreat, for example, a British unit withdrawing from the Flesquières salient came to a large, deserted house. Thinking it was safely out of the enemy's reach, they decided to take shelter there for the night. Except for their weapons, the men left all their equipment on some wire beds in the cellar, where they planned to sleep, and stood talking in relaxed groups in the courtyard.

One officer felt somehow uneasy. "I cannot say," he related "what prompted me to wander out of the gates and down the road. It was there I heard some Germans talking quietly to one another. I was so dumbfounded that I thought at first it was some of our own people joking, but it was unmistakable, and I hurried back with my warning. No one would believe me, of course. . . ."

Still, the men were placed in a rough position of defense as a precaution, and a runner was dispatched to alert another unit close by. Just when the officer's companions were beginning to think that his story was the wild tale of a man exhausted from the long strain of battle, the Germans began to call out to one another. Immediately, without waiting for an order to fire, a nervous machine gunner blazed away in the direction of their voices, and a nasty little fight was on.

The British were badly outnumbered. If they remained in the vicinity of the house more than a minute or two longer, they were done for. Making a hasty exit in the darkness, they had to leave behind not only the equipment in the cellar but several wounded men who could not be moved. With real heroism, the American doctor caring for the wounded refused to desert them, and was presumably taken prisoner.

Events of this sort were not unusual, for fixed battle lines no longer existed and the country was unfamiliar to most. Staffs had by now lost any real touch with the units they commanded. Lacking definite orders, men usually followed the path of least resistance and joined the endless columns fleeing from the front. Major Gibbs, who had escaped with his guns and most of his men, reported that "the main roads and every little crossroad as far as the eye could carry were all massed with moving troops going back." In general, they headed in a southwesterly direction, though nobody seemed

to have any notion where they would stop, or where a new stand—if any—would be made. In spite of the chaos, the retreat was for the most part an orderly one.

The British rout continued; and now civilians far behind the original battle line were caught up in it. "The roads were full . . . of refugees," Major Gibbs remembered; "women, old men, girls and children, with what possessions they could load into a farm wagon piled sky high. They pulled their cattle along by chains or ropes tied around their horns. Some of them pushed perambulators full of packages and carried their babies. Others staggered under bundles. . . ."

At the same time, however, French troops began to appear in ever greater numbers, especially on the southern flank. But as yet there were not enough of them to affect the course of the battle. Gibbs remembered passing over one ridge where a rear guard of blue-clad French infantry had dug rifle pits every few yards. Waiting for the enemy, the men sat and smoked in their holes, which seemed to the Englishmen "so like half-dug graves." And that, doubtless, was what they soon would be.

By the end of the week some troops had retired as much as forty miles. Ominously now, the road signs were pointing to Paris.

French soldiers join the desperate fighting on the Somme line

CHAPTER FIVE

A Bold Move

War Council

On the afternoon of Tuesday, March 26th—the sixth day of the "Michael" attack—convoys of heavily guarded staff cars drew up in front of the old town hall in the hamlet of Doullens. The town lay just to the west of the battle—close enough for gunfire to be heard at all times.

Tanks patrolled the approaches to Doullens; for the men who emerged from the cars were some of the foremost political and military leaders of France and Britain. They would have made a rich prize for any marauding Germans.

In this moment of crisis they had called an emergency war council. Raymond Poincaré, the president of France, was there, and the nation's premier, Georges Clemenceau. Representing the military were General Henri Philippe Pétain, commander in chief of the French Army, and his dynamic chief of staff, General Ferdinand Foch. Field Marshal Douglas Haig, Pétain's opposite number with the British forces, had come down from his headquarters in the north, bringing his army commanders with him. Only General Gough was absent. His army, as such, had ceased to exist, and he was soon to be relieved of his command.

These men were meeting in a desperate effort to resolve the differences that had long prevented any real cooperation between the armies of the two nations on the Western Front. Never had the division built up by the mutual distrust of the leaders of these two armies been so open or so dangerous.

In the days just past, when the outnumbered British had reeled backward under the staggering impact of the German offensive, Pétain had been miserly indeed with French help. He had his reasons. He was obsessed with the fear that the "Michael" offensive was merely a diversion—that Ludendorff would yet deliver his main blow against the French forces to the east between Soissons and Rheims. He refused to make any move that would weaken his own line. As the situation grew worse, Pétain had given Haig the distinct impression that he intended to abandon the British to their fate, while his armies fell back to cover all possible approaches to Paris.

Such was the background of the Doullens meeting. It hardly made for a favorable beginning. As Haig entered the town hall, where the conference was to take place, Pétain confided to Clemenceau, "There is a man who will be forced to see his army surrender in the open field within a fortnight." Then he added grimly, "We'll be very lucky if we're not obliged to do the same." For the Allies, this was perhaps the low point of the war.

Then Haig made a bold move that instantly seemed to change everything. He proposed that one man be elevated to the supreme command of all Allied armies on the Western Front. Moreover, that man would be a Frenchman. Haig named General Foch. It was a masterstroke. Haig was no longer denied the help he needed.

One other important decision was made that day. The

"Michael" offensive must be stopped before it reached the great rail junction of Amiens, now a bare twenty miles away from the most advanced German units. The danger was as clear as the need to do something about it. Once Ludendorff captured this town and moved beyond it, he would have effectively severed connections between the British and the French.

To arrest German progress at Amiens—or at any other spot short of the English Channel—may have seemed to some that afternoon an impossible undertaking. But not to Foch. Rising to speak to the leaders assembled at Doullens, he said: "It is a hard task you offer me now: a compromised situation, a crumbling front, an adverse battle in full progress. Nevertheless I accept."

Foch

Calm yet forceful, self-assured, and inspiring—these words reveal a measure of the magnetic energy of General Foch. He was a short, bandy-legged man with small bright eyes, a sweeping moustache, and a wide, easy smile. His face had an almost unnatural intensity about it, as if a constant fever burned inside him. At sixty-six, Foch was somewhat older than most of the leading figures of the war, and until this moment it had appeared that the best years of his military career were behind him.

No one had championed with more zeal—or with more recklessness—the notion that victory could be achieved only by repeated attack, no matter what the cost. Unfortunately, Foch had been in large part responsible for the massive, costly, battering-ram assaults launched against the Germans in the early days of trench warfare on the Western Front;

as public discontent with the way the struggle was being handled mounted in France, nervous politicians had found him a ready scapegoat. And yet, it was not surprising that the same men who had lately sought to deprive him of his power and influence should now turn to Foch as their savior. They might recognize, perhaps, that his mind had none of the inventiveness of his crafty adversary, Ludendorff; but they knew also that Foch had another quality that Ludendorff lacked altogether—the ability, by his own emotional intensity, to inspire men to prodigious efforts when the going was worst and the future looked most bleak.

Foch often said, "A battle won is a battle we will not acknowledge to be lost." In these days of trial, it was a motto that would hearten the hard-pressed Allies.

The "Mars" Attack

Ludendorff himself was beginning to have his share of troubles. The unexpected resistance he encountered along the line from the Flesquières salient to Arras had completely upset his timetable. The great wheel-around to the northwest, which should have been under way days ago, had not even begun. If it was delayed much longer, this key move in Ludendorff's scheme would have to be abandoned, simply because his troops would be too exhausted to continue.

The southern thrust of his attack, however—which had been intended as nothing more than a holding operation—was succeeding beyond his wildest expectations. Ludendorff was thus presented with a dilemma for which he was quite unprepared. Should he now forsake his original plan and shift the main weight of the "Michael" offensive to its south flank, with Amiens his new goal? Or should he attempt to press the northern attack on an even larger scale, with fresh troops, in the hope of regaining his lost initiative?

Ludendorff wavered. The "robot Napoleon" was paralyzed by an indecisiveness such as he had never before experienced. And it was in this state of mind that he committed the first really great blunder of his career.

Ludendorff had made plans for a series of follow-up attacks in the event "Michael" ran into difficulties. At dawn on the eighth day, March 28th, the first of these, called "Mars," smashed like a piledriver against the defenses of Arras. The immediate objective was to capture that fortress city, which would crack the British line at its strongest point. Orders called for a follow-up advance to Boulogne on the English Channel coast, seventy-two miles by road from Arras! No hope could have been more vain.

Camouflaged French guns move south to aid the Allies near Arras

This time the British were ready. Warned that an attack might be coming, many units withdrew from their positions in the Forward Zone, so that when the German bombardment began, it fell on empty trenches. Nor was there fog to hide the movements of the attackers. British artillery poured fire on the trenches and shell holes where Ludendorff's infantry was assembling. The Germans, crippled by recent losses among their picked storm troops, could not rely on infiltration; thus they were forced to revert to the old methods of mass assault. Wave after wave, in some places shoulder to shoulder six lines deep, advanced through a pouring rain, in full view of their enemies, and were decimated by artillery and machine-gun fire.

That day, Ludendorff sent forward thirteen divisions, or nearly 200,000 men. Along most of the front, his attack barely dented the British Battle Zone. The Germans had suffered one of their worst defeats of the entire war. In the evening, Ludendorff called off the attack.

So "Mars" came to an end, after a violent but brief career. From that moment on, it must have been clear to Ludendorff that "Michael's" days, too, were numbered. Arras had proved to be a rock that shivered the hammer of Mars.

Ludendorff's failure to capture Arras meant that his cherished plan for victory in a single stroke had to be abandoned once for all. There would be no majestic turn and sweep of German armies to the northwest, no roll-up of the Allied line, no hounding of a scattered and beaten enemy into the sea, no Paris by April.

But Ludendorff was not done with "Michael" yet. Perhaps he could still salvage something from the wreckage of his hopes—something more, that is, than the vast stretches of dead land that had so far proved his only real conquest.

LUDENDORFF IN ACTION

MARCH, 1918. Ludendorff's mighty assault begins according to plan. At 4:40 on the morning of the 21st, six thousand pieces of German artillery open up on the British front with a crash. Deadly gas poisons the air. German gunners train their fire on British artillery positions, then shorten their range to cut down the men in the trenches. At 9:40 the barrage lets up. German storm troops rise to their feet. Some sixty divisions, from Lens to La Fère, surge forward for the kill.

The first day is a disaster for the British. The German Seventeenth and Second armies press on against the British Third, under General Julian H. G. Byng. The German Eighteenth Army overruns General Hubert Gough's Fifth Army, reaching the Crozat Canal on the second day. Gough's four divisions are no match for the enemy's twenty-four divisions.

However, on the morning of the third day, March 23rd, the British Third Army offers fierce resistance. Ludendorff's Seventeenth and Second armies are being halted. Only the Eighteenth Army continues to make its spectacular advance in the south.

A CHANGE IN PLAN. Ludendorff suddenly decides on a change of tactics. His southern armies are doing far better than expected. Those to the north are no longer advancing according to plan. He issues new orders. He spreads the weight of the attack over the whole area, thrusting not only to the northwest but also to the west and southwest.

Ludendorff now hopes to engage and destroy French-held positions at the same time that he destroys the British.

At Doullens, however, just behind the lines, the Allied High Command meets and agrees to unite under the direction of General Foch. Ludendorff for the first time faces a coordinated defense. By April 4th, although Ludendorff has control of the river Somme and the surrounding area, the important rail center of Amiens remains beyond his grasp. His casualties have been enormous, and the survivors are exhausted. The enemy has not been destroyed. New divisions from America will soon begin to pour into the front lines, lending new strength to the Allied cause.

In effect, the battle is over. While other battles will be fought, Ludendorff's once formidable armies will never be the same. He has lost his great gamble for victory.

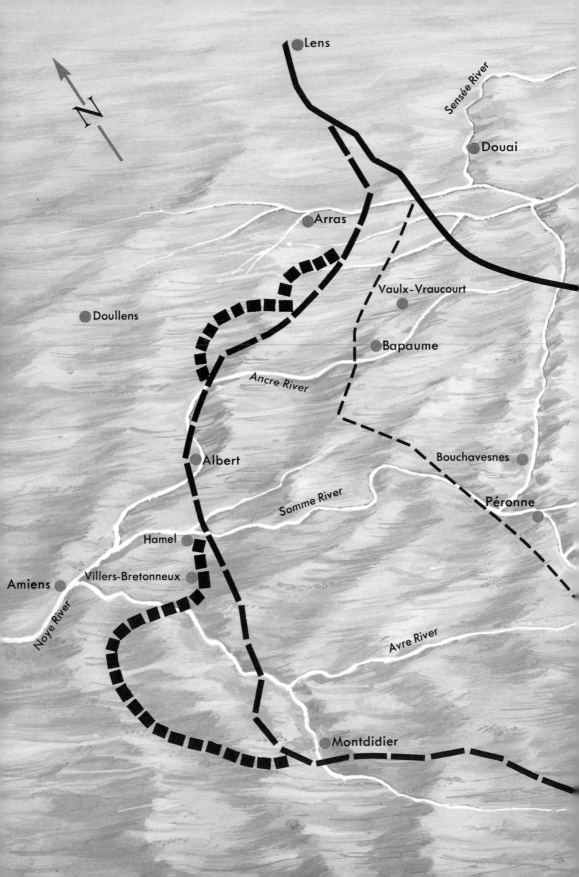

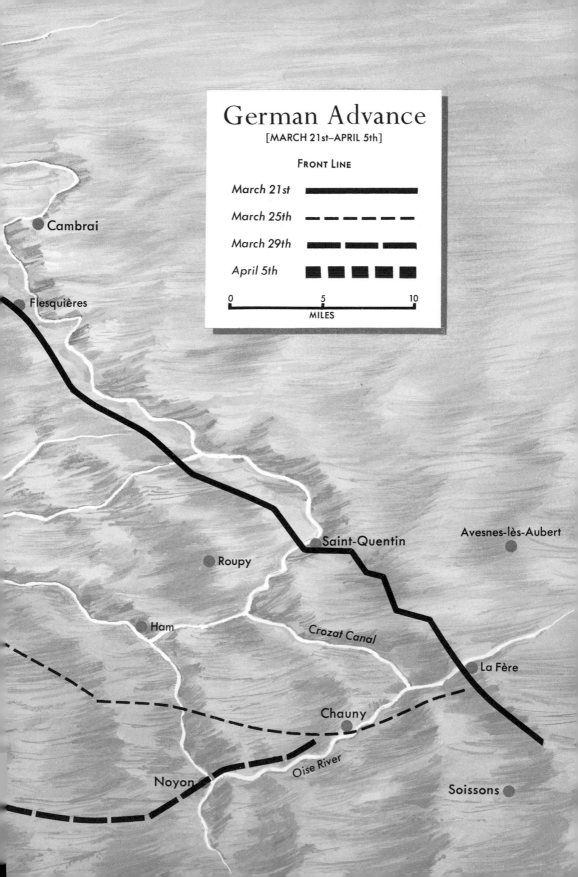

German Advance
[MARCH 21st–APRIL 5th]

FRONT LINE

March 21st ——————

March 25th — — — —

March 29th ▬ ▬ ▬ ▬

April 5th ■ ■ ■ ■ ■

0   5   10
MILES

Cambrai

Flesquières

Avesnes-lès-Aubert

Saint-Quentin

Roupy

Ham

Crozat Canal

La Fère

Chauny

Noyon

Oise River

Soissons

A New Target: Amiens

As a last resort, Ludendorff turned his efforts to a new, if more limited, goal. He decided to concentrate on capturing the rail center of Amiens.

But the farther Ludendorff's armies got from their original line of attack, the more difficult it was to supply them. As they passed into the region of the old Somme battlefields, that task became overpowering. Roads, if they existed at all, had been badly torn up in the fighting. When heavy rains began to fall toward the end of the month, they became even more impassable, turning into deep rivers of mud.

Where the British and the French could not stop Ludendorff's armies, hunger and exhaustion did. Men who had been fighting day and night for a week could not be expected to go on indefinitely. Worse, they were not always sure of being fed. There is an old saying that an army travels on its belly, and along the Western Front the Germans were advancing on a pitifully empty one.

"We are glad if ration carts can get up to us at night; then men and horses feed for the next 24 hours at one sitting," an officer named Rudolf Binding reported in his diary. Too, in a land where most streams were dangerously polluted and wells wrecked or poisoned, thirst was no less a problem. "Often there is no water even for washing, let alone drinking," Binding wrote. "All that is available is the icy-cold water of the shell-holes, quite clear above the green scum at the bottom. We first take a mouthful each to drink, and then use it successively for cleaning our teeth, then moistening for our shaving-brushes, and finally for washing.

"I can still find no word nor image to express the awfulness of that waste," Binding later noted. "There is nothing like it on earth, nor can be." Where there once had been villages, now only a few blackened stumps of trees remained, standing "like corpses upright."

In some places, even the ruins were ruined. "Yesterday," Binding wrote in his entry for March 26th, "I was looking for Bouchavesnes, which used to be quite a large place. There was nothing but a board nailed to a low post with the inscription in English, 'This was Bouchavesnes.'" Not a blade of grass nor a green leaf was to be seen. "The layer of soil which once covered the loose chalk is now buried underneath it. Thousands of shells have brought the stones to the surface and smothered the earth with its own entrails. . . ."

Then Binding added an afterthought, and it was the remark of a man who had been through too much war to find glory in it any longer: "This area ought to remain as it is," he said. "No road, no well, no settlement ought to be made here, and every ruler, leading statesman, or president of a republic ought to be brought to see it, instead of swearing an oath on the Constitution, henceforth and forever. Then there would be no more wars."

The Turning Point

As Ludendorff's mighty offensive began to run down, the struggle became brutally sluggish and somehow unreal, like a nightmare in slow motion. Men moved as though in a trance, and behaved in ways that were increasingly unpredictable, often unsoldierly, and sometimes strange. The *Official History* records instances when dead-tired British rear-guard units retired at a slow walk, while the Germans followed at the same pace and in plain view a few thousand yards away. When the British lay down, the Germans halted;

A strangely peaceful trench abandoned by the Germans in April, 1918, when the "Michael" offensive had come to a dismal halt

attack was apparently out of the question: "They too were tired, and possibly hungrier; there was little artillery support for them, and without it the German infantry did not seem inclined to face fire."

And so, Ludendorff's men lost one glittering opportunity after another.

On the night of March 27th, in the south, just beyond the town of Montdidier, a great gap nine miles wide suddenly opened between the British and French as the two armies retreated on divergent lines. For several hours it remained almost completely empty, an invitation to the enemy. In that time, the Germans could have gone right through, as unmolested as hikers on a country stroll. The two Allied armies would have been separated. If that had happened, who could say what the result might have been? Could the fragile line still have been reestablished? Or would the French have swung back toward Paris, allowing the Germans to pour through past Amiens to the sea?

But the Germans had no cavalry to exploit the situation. Their infantry had stopped to rest. By the next morning, the hole had been plugged by reinforcements that the French had hastily thrown into the line. A heavy, deadening rain was falling. That afternoon the Allies mounted a small attack of their own in this sector, and managed to push the Germans back a couple of miles. It was an action of little immediate importance, and much of the ground gained was soon lost again. But coming at the very moment that Ludendorff was halting his ill-fated "Mars" offensive in front of Arras, this show of fighting spirit on the part of the Allies was a bad omen for the future of "Michael."

Thursday, March 28th, seems to have been the real turning point in the battle. Not only had Ludendorff failed to take

Arras and to exploit the gap at Montdidier; he was also losing control of his army.

On that same day Rudolf Binding witnessed a scene that was ominous testimony to the breakdown of the German army's morale.

As Binding drove into the town of Albert, a base twenty miles to the northeast of Amiens, he saw German soldiers behaving in a curious fashion. "There were men driving cows before them on a line; others who carried a hen under one arm and a box of notepaper under the other. Men carrying a bottle of wine under one arm and another open in the other hand. Men who had torn a silk drawing-room curtain from its rod were dragging it to the rear as a bit of loot. More men with writing-paper and colored note-books. Evidently they had found it desirable to sack a stationer's shop. Men dressed up in comic disguise. Men with top hats on their heads. Men staggering. Men who could hardly walk."

This outburst of drunkenness and senseless looting by the Germans was the pitiful result of three and a half years' deprivation, and month after month of existence on starvation rations. Binding could understand the causes. He could sympathize with these men. But he could also foresee the disastrous results. Every moment wasted gave the enemy that much more time to dig in, to bring up reinforcements, and to restore his shattered fortunes.

"The troops which moved out of Albert next day cheered with wine and in victorious spirits," Binding related, "were mown down straight away on the railway embankment by a few English machine guns, while those who escaped were laid out by French artillery in their next attack."

Amiens still remained just out of reach, but so close that

it tantalized Ludendorff and lured him into making renewed, and ever more hopeless, attacks. On the 29th, the ninth day of the German offensive, an ice-cold rain again fell steadily all through the day, and a lull in the fighting settled along most of the line. Both sides dug in, a sure sign that the old, stalemated type of warfare was returning.

Many German troops were beginning to display a reluctance to expose themselves to fire. Under the circumstances, this attitude was understandable. On the sector just to the south of the river Somme, for instance, Ludendorff called for a general attack. For some unknown reason, the German divisions confined their actions here to a single raid of little military importance.

Near the village of Hamel, a detachment of infantry moved forward to occupy a trench on a small hill. No sooner had they done so than a squadron of British cavalry rode up to within three hundred yards, dismounted, fixed bayonets, and began to walk up the slope. The Germans scurried away without firing back. It was not like them. . . .

"The power of attack was exhausted. Spirits sank to zero," one German soldier admitted. But Ludendorff refused to call a halt. "Michael" must go on. Amiens must be taken. On March 30th he ordered a renewal of the offensive on a twenty-five-mile front from the Somme south to Montdidier. In places military police had to drive the men forward at pistol point.

Almost immediately the fighting collapsed into a weary and disjointed mauling back and forth over the ruins of some village or an insignificant patch of woodland. The Germans managed to gain a mile or two, and pushed across the river Avre in several places, but by the next day, Easter Sunday, the attack had sputtered out.

Death of "Michael"

Now even Ludendorff knew that his troops had to rest. For three days, from the 1st to the 3rd of April, the battle died down completely, except for a raid here and there and persistent artillery fire. Both sides worked frantically to bring up reinforcements and reorganize their divisions. They dug more trenches while the rain continued. The area before Amiens became, in the words of Hamilton Gibbs, a "mud patch broken by shell holes." Covered by tarpaulins that never quite kept the water out, men shivered in slimy burrows and tried to catch a few moments of sleep.

On April 4th, Ludendorff made a last, desperate attempt to take Amiens. It seemed doomed from the beginning. "More and more reports trickled in of fresh enemy divisions springing up round the fragile salient which had been won," wrote one German historian. "More and more artillery fire swelled in volume; higher and higher rose the losses of the Germans in dead, wounded and sick, and more and more did the spirit of their attack evaporate."

And yet, with an incredibly dogged persistence, Ludendorff's troops dragged themselves out of their newly dug trenches and once more hurled their tired bodies at the machine guns and massed artillery of the British and French. There was rain, as usual. Men slipped and fell in the mud, guns clogged, and the sodden landscape became littered with corpses. "The physical exhaustion of the infantry . . . was so great," Rudolf Binding remarked, "that finally the men could hardly fire their rifles. They let themselves be slowly wiped out by the enemy's artillery fire almost without caring, and would hardly move from the spot. They were just like used-up horses which . . . dumbly take the blows of the whip without a movement. They could not advance; they could not shoot; they could not even get out of the way of fire; they just stuck there."

The situation was hopeless. On the night of April 5th, Ludendorff called off the attack. From the outskirts of a tiny village called Villers-Bretonneux, the farthest point of the German advance, the high spires of the cathedral of Amiens were clearly visible, nine miles in the distance. That was as close as Ludendorff would ever get.

An exploding 38 cm. cannon shell blasts a Battle Zone position

*Arrival of American
troops in France*

CHAPTER SIX

Last Days of the War

Success or Failure?

"Michael" had come to a halt.

The greatest attack of the First World War had run its course. In just 16 days, Ludendorff's three armies had conquered some 1,200 square miles of enemy-held territory. That was more than the Allies had won in 44 months of fighting on the Western Front. Their trophies of battle also included some 90,000 prisoners and 1,100 guns, along with vast quantities of supplies.

But in the long view of history, Ludendorff's achievement loses much of its luster. To begin with, he accomplished not a single one of his announced objectives. The British Army had not been destroyed. The British and the French had not been split apart. Not even Amiens had been taken. What, then, had actually been gained? The Germans had simply reoccupied their old battlefields and the regions they had laid waste a year earlier.

Worse, Ludendorff now had fifty extra miles of front to hold; it would prove more a liability than an asset. This was a great, ugly bulge that not only was impossible to fortify in any real strength but also presented badly exposed flanks.

German losses in killed, wounded, and captured were only a little more than the combined casualties of the British and French—an estimated 348,000 as opposed to perhaps 330,000. But they could much less afford them. By the spring of 1918, a man lost to the Germans was a man who could not be replaced. The Allies, on the other hand, could soon count on hundreds of thousands of fresh and eager American troops who were already arriving on French soil.

The menace of a total German breakthrough had, moreover, brought the faction-ridden British and French together at last. Once they could cooperate, they could hold. Part of Ludendorff's gamble had been that they would not.

In the end, "Michael" must be classed as a brilliant failure. As far as Germany's hopes for winning the war were concerned, it was a major setback. But Ludendorff was not done yet. On April 9th, just four days after "Michael" had finally subsided, he struck the British again, this time to the north along the valley of the river Lys.

Another Near Miss

It was the story of "Michael" all over again, but on a somewhat smaller scale: an intense early-morning bombardment followed by the rapid advance of infiltrating storm troops through a thick fog. This time the main force of the attack fell on a weak division of Portuguese troops that broke and ran, leaving a huge gap for the Germans to stream through. Back and back swung the British line. For a time the situation looked so dark the preliminary orders were given for the evacuation and demolition of the port of Calais. Preparations were even made for the flooding of the low-lying area along the French coast west of Dunkerque.

Sudden and shocking death comes to a German infantry soldier

While the British could afford to fall back forty or fifty miles in the "Michael" attack, a loss of twenty or thirty miles now would press them into the sea. The peril was great; Sir Douglas Haig felt impelled to issue an appeal to his troops that has since become historic: "Many of us now are tired," he wrote in his General Order of the Day for April 12th. "To those I would say that victory will belong to the side which holds out the longest. . . . There is no other course open to us but to fight it out! Every position must be held to the last man: there must be no retirement. With our backs to the wall and believing in the justice of our cause, each one of us must fight on to the end. The safety of our Homes and the Freedom of mankind alike depend upon the conduct of each one of us at this critical moment."

Whether the British could have held out alone it is difficult to say. In the end, it is probable they could, for something had gone out of Ludendorff's troops since the March offensive. They were tired, too. After the failure of "Michael," many of them must have begun to doubt the possibility of victory. Once again discipline relaxed, and there were widespread looting and drunkenness during some of the most critical moments of the battle. Nor was Ludendorff at his best. He missed one opportunity after another to exploit weaknesses in the British line, and seemed overcome by the same confusion that had plagued him in March.

At any event, halfway through this twenty-day struggle on the plains of Flanders, French reserves began to arrive. While Haig might complain mightily about Foch's stinginess with reinforcements, the fact is that they strengthened the wavering Allied line immensely. Now, too, whole American divisions were moving into quiet sectors of the Western Front. More French troops were thus released to help the British. By the end of April, the German offensive on the Lys was done for, and again victory had escaped their grasp.

The Black Day of the German Army

A month passed. Time was running out on Ludendorff now. Then, late in May, he made his third great gamble for victory. His blow fell along a steep, hog-backed ridge called the Chemin des Dames, a position the Allies considered so impregnable that they used it mainly as a rest area. In a massive surprise attack, he hurled the better part of two armies against seven undermanned British and French divisions holding a quiet sector of the line just to the east of the bulge left by "Michael" two months earlier. Ludendorff overran it in a single morning. By the 1st of June, five days after his offensive began, he had reached the river Marne at Château-Thierry; Paris was only thirty-seven miles away.

It was 1914 all over again. For a few hours, nothing seemed to bar Ludendorff's way to the French capital. But his opportunity proved to be an illusion. Not only were his troops too exhausted to continue the advance, but now the very thing he had gambled on forestalling had happened. In the lines opposing his sagging divisions, thousands of fresh American troops were beginning to appear.

The scene was unforgettable, one of those rare moments in history of high drama, when nations rise or fall and the world is forever altered. Dispirited Allied troops who had for days known only defeat and retreat suddenly witnessed the heartening spectacle of swarms of Americans thronging forward toward the front. "They passed in endless columns," one French staff officer remembered, "closely packed in motor lorries, with their feet in the air in extraordinary attitudes, some perched on the tarpaulins, almost all bareheaded and bare-chested, singing American songs at the top of their voices amid the cheers of the onlookers. The spectacle of these magnificent youths from across the sea, these beardless children of twenty, radiating strength and health . . . produced a great effect."

Now even dour Pétain blossomed with confidence. "If we can hold on to the end of June," he prophesied, "our situation will be excellent. In July we can resume the offensive; after that, victory is ours." Pétain's prediction was to prove a remarkably accurate one—if, for the moment, Ludendorff refused to see the truth of it. The strength of the German armies was ebbing by the day; their morale was crumbling, and it was plain that they had reached the limit of their endurance. And yet, the "robot Napoleon" hardly paused to contemplate the wreckage of his hopes. He was too busy preparing for fresh offensives. One more time he attacked, trying to break out of the Château-Thierry salient, and one more time he was stopped. He had managed to gain very little ground at an exceedingly high cost; what he had won he was soon forced to give up.

That final, and most disastrous, of Ludendorff's gambles lasted for three days in the middle of July. Hardly was the battle over when, true to Pétain's word, the Allies began to hit back. Their first counterblow fell around the perimeter of the Château-Thierry salient. It presented Ludendorff with an abrupt and unpleasant choice: if he did not retreat from a dangerously exposed position, thousands of irreplaceable men might be caught in a trap.

He retreated.

There was worse to come. On the 8th of August, 14 divisions of Australian and Canadian infantry, 3 divisions of cavalry, more than 2,000 guns, and some 450 tanks smashed the German line along the Amiens front—the very place where Ludendorff's great "Michael" offensive had stalled back in April. The attack came without warning, and it was devastating. In a single day, the Allied troops penetrated almost 8 miles, and took 334 guns and 13,000 prisoners. But the loss of men, or ground, or matériel was not what really mattered to the Germans that day. It was something else far more important, far more ominous. At Amiens, the once-formidable fighting spirit of the German Army had completely disintegrated.

Behind the German lines, retreating troops greeted reserve units going up to the front with abuse and jeers. Men surrendered willingly, almost eagerly. Winston Churchill, once more a witness of great events, saw streams of German prisoners filing back along the dusty summer roads of Picardy. "The woebegone expressions of the officers," he commented, "contrasted sharply with the almost cheerful countenances of the rank and file."

"August 8th," Ludendorff would later write, "was the black day of the German Army in the history of the war. . . . It put the decline of our fighting powers beyond all doubt."

Where "Michael" had ended, Allied victory had begun.

Under Foch's direction, Allied attacks increased in intensity through the rest of the summer and into the fall. As they gradually spread in an almost continuous line from one end of the Western Front to the other, the German Army gave way, little by little. It was finished, and so was Ludendorff. On October 26, 1918, the Kaiser asked for his resignation. Three weeks later, Germany capitulated, and the First World War was over.

German Forces
March 1918

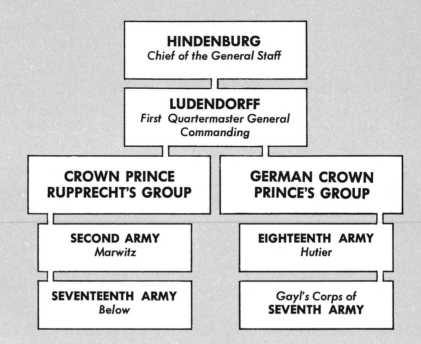

HINDENBURG
Chief of the General Staff

LUDENDORFF
First Quartermaster General Commanding

CROWN PRINCE RUPPRECHT'S GROUP

GERMAN CROWN PRINCE'S GROUP

SECOND ARMY
Marwitz

EIGHTEENTH ARMY
Hutier

SEVENTEENTH ARMY
Below

Gayl's Corps of **SEVENTH ARMY**

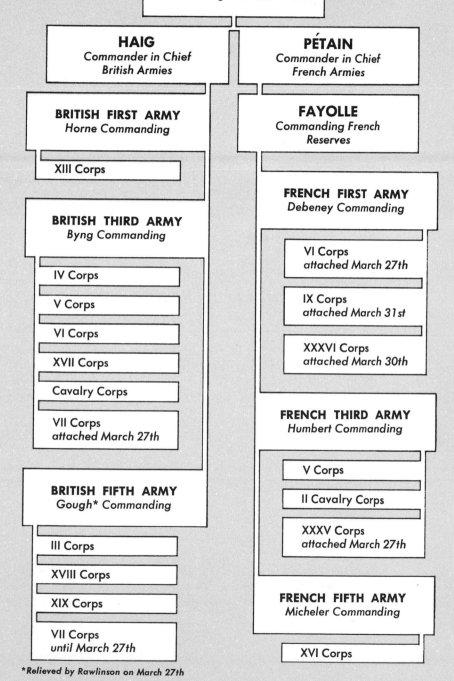

Allied Forces
March 1918

FOCH
Commanding after March 27th

HAIG
*Commander in Chief
British Armies*

PÉTAIN
*Commander in Chief
French Armies*

BRITISH FIRST ARMY
Horne Commanding

XIII Corps

FAYOLLE
*Commanding French
Reserves*

BRITISH THIRD ARMY
Byng Commanding

IV Corps

V Corps

VI Corps

XVII Corps

Cavalry Corps

VII Corps
attached March 27th

FRENCH FIRST ARMY
Debeney Commanding

VI Corps
attached March 27th

IX Corps
attached March 31st

XXXVI Corps
attached March 30th

FRENCH THIRD ARMY
Humbert Commanding

V Corps

II Cavalry Corps

XXXV Corps
attached March 27th

BRITISH FIFTH ARMY
Gough* Commanding

III Corps

XVIII Corps

XIX Corps

VII Corps
until March 27th

FRENCH FIFTH ARMY
Micheler Commanding

XVI Corps

*Relieved by Rawlinson on March 27th

For Further Reading

Nonfiction

CHAPMAN, GUY (editor). *Vain Glory.* London: Cassell, 1937.

CRUTTWELL, CHARLES R. M. F. *A History of the Great War, 1914–1918.* Oxford: Clarendon, 1940.

FALLS, CYRIL. *The Great War: 1914–1918.* New York: Putnam, 1959.

LIDDELL HART, B. H. *German Generals Talk.* New York: Morrow, 1948.

NICHOLLS, T. B. *Official History of the War.* London: Macmillan, 1935.

PITT, BARRIE. *1918–The Last Act.* New York: Norton, 1963.

READ, HERBERT. *In Retreat: A Journal of the Retreat of the Fifth Army from St. Quentin, March, 1918.* London: Woolf, 1925.

REEDER, RED. *Story of the First World War.* New York: Duell, Sloan & Pearce, 1962.

STALLINGS, LAURENCE. *The First World War.* New York: Simon & Schuster, 1933.

Fiction

ALTSHELER, JOSEPH A. *Guns of Europe.* New York: Appleton-Century, 1959.

DOS PASSOS, JOHN. *Three Soldiers.* New York: Modern Library.

FENNER, PHYLLIS (compiler). *Over There.* New York: Morrow, 1961.

NORDHOFF, CHARLES and HALL, JAMES N. *Falcons of France.* Boston: Atlantic Monthly Press, 1929.

REMARQUE, ERICH M. *All Quiet on the Western Front.* New York: Fawcett.

Index